you
already
have
the
answers

**365 Questions
to Reveal
Your Greatest
Strengths**

A GRATITUDE JOURNAL

you
already
have
the
answers

Amanda Deibert

CHRONICLE BOOKS

SAN FRANCISCO

INTRODUCTION

The concept of this guided journal is right in the title: *You Already Have the Answers*. You've been through hard things, and you kept going. You've done things other people didn't think were possible. You've loved fiercely, and you've experienced painful losses. You may even be going through something difficult right now. I want you to know that you are not alone.

That is why this journal is not going to be full of promises that you can wish away your problems with the power of positive thinking. You have been through too much and done too much work to not get credit for navigating the tough parts of life. That's what this journal is about. It is ultimately a love letter to you—from me, yes, but also from you. We are going to honor your experiences, good and bad, together. You have hopes, desires, and special gifts that are just waiting to pour out of you—and you already have coping mechanisms in place for when life goes sideways. To help you access all of that, this journal asks carefully cultivated questions designed to remind you of powerful moments along your life's journey, guiding you to unlock talents and strengths you might not be fully using so that you can rediscover yourself in a more complete way.

This concept may seem simple, and it is. It is also life changing. I know because I've watched it happen in real time over the last six years. I started asking these kinds of questions as a bit of an experiment on Twitter. The experiment accidentally became a social media movement that is still going strong. The results were beyond my wildest expectations. I thought I would ask a few questions, and maybe a handful of people would answer. Instead, after just a couple of weeks, my questions garnered hundreds of thousands of replies. As the Twitter threads went viral, people expressed empathy and connected with one another—and their lives were changed. I received countless stories from those who reconnected with old friends or took new risks, all because of the questions I posed. People have shared how these questions helped them realize their true passions, switch jobs, and start new relationships. The questions have even offered perspective and hope to people becoming caretakers or mourning the loss of loved ones. One man, who lives in another country, told me that answering these questions every day over the course of a year changed his negative view about people in the LGBTQIA+ community. When I started this experiment, I had no idea how impactful these questions would be, but the truth is that a simple question, asked the right way, can change your mindset. And answering powerful questions every day will change your life.

That's exactly what this journal is designed to do. Each chapter is part of a monthlong theme, but you may start it any time of the year. Because I want you to know that I am with you every step of the way, I even share some of my own, deeply personal, answers to the questions.

The sharing can also be really healing and powerful. You absolutely don't have to share any of your answers with anyone else to have a life-changing experience, but you might be surprised by what happens when you do. So, feel free to bring this journal into your book club or friend group. Check in with each other once a month and share one or two of your favorite answers. It will increase intimacy and reveal things about even your closest loved ones that you never knew. The questions may also uncover cherished memories that lead you to reach out to people from long ago in your life.

This process is going to be positive—and fun! Thank you for allowing me to be with you on this journey.

CHAPTER 1

what
you're
already
doing
right

One of the most difficult things for many of us to do is be kind to ourselves. I was raised in a very religious, conservative, Southern household where the message, especially for little girls, was: don't exist—but if you *MUST* exist, you'd better apologize for it immediately. "I'm sorry" is one of my most uttered phrases. I'm telling you this because, even right now, I feel the urge to apologize to you for starting the book with this chapter because it asks you to do the hardest thing: talk about the ways in which you are strong and brave. Share the tremendous things you have been through and survived, and the risks you've taken that paid off. (It's also a time to celebrate the times those risks *didn't* pay off and you *KEPT GOING ANYWAY*.)

Here's the part that has me squirming: I can't suggest you do that if I don't do it myself. So, to avoid being a hypocrite, I am going to share that side of me with you. We'll go through this vulnerable process together.

One of the best things I ever did was "kidnap" a teenager when I was twenty. Let me explain: My mother died when I was fourteen and my two younger sisters were nine and eight. My mother's death was difficult and traumatic, and it was made even worse by the period that followed. After years of abuse and more tragedy, I was separated from my sisters (they are my half-siblings, which added complications) when I was seventeen. I spent years trying to get in contact with them, to no avail, until finally, in my freshman year of college, my very sweet roommate agreed to spend her fall break taking a road trip with me from North Carolina to Florida, where my sisters lived. My roommate and I held a little stakeout down the street from my old home. We intercepted my sisters getting off the bus from middle school. I took them on a walk and gave them money, a scarf that had belonged to our mother, and, most important, my phone number.

Two years later, I got the call. One of my sisters had run away from home and needed shelter. I jumped into my little Dodge Neon with my then-girlfriend, who had made us a road-trip mix CD appropriately titled *Kidnapping a Teenager*. We drove to the Georgia border, where we met my sister and her boyfriend. We threw her belongings in the trunk of my car and drove back to North Carolina, where I made it just in time to take my final exams. I called my sister's father and told him that she was going to live with me. He said, "Jesus Christ," then, "Okay," and hung up. My friends, roommates, and girlfriend quickly assembled furniture and a community to take in my sister. I was financially on my own, but I'd managed to scrape together an apartment, a job, and a decent academic scholarship, so I was more than happy to provide a home for my sister. The tale of what happened after is long and complicated, but my kidnapping-a-teenager story explains a lot about who I am as a person.

I share this because moments like these have taught me who I really am at my core. I know I'm the kind of woman who will do anything to protect the people I love, even if it comes at a personal risk or cost. I know I am resilient and a fighter. I know I am not afraid to stand up to bullies. I know I'm capable. If I am honest with myself, I can't argue against those facts, because they have been proven. Knowing these things about myself has served me so many times in my life.

You have lessons like this too. You have been through some shit, and you're still here. You have so many stories of triumph and struggle and endurance to celebrate. So let's do that. This isn't a book about what you should be doing better; this is a journal to help you celebrate all the things you are doing right!

What is a risk
you've taken that
has really paid off?

_____

_____

_____

_____

_____

What is the most
meaningful compliment
someone has ever
given you?

_____

_____

_____

_____

_____

Write about
something you are
proud of right now.

_____

_____

_____

_____

What is a kind thing
you did for someone
else that ended up
meaning a lot to you?

_____

_____

_____

_____

How have you grown as a person in the last year?

Write about
a time you
were brave.

If you could write a
love letter to your
younger self, what
would it say?

What is
something you
are proud to
have overcome?

_____

_____

_____

_____

What keeps
you feeling
grounded?

_____

_____

_____

_____

Have you ever had a
moment in your life that
tested your morals?
How did you react?
Did you do what you
thought you would?

What is an
experience you
are glad to be
done with?

_____

_____

_____

_____

Describe a
time you felt
truly attractive.

_____

_____

_____

_____

When do you feel the
most comfortable in
your own skin?

_____

_____

_____

_____

What is your
favorite physical
activity?

_____

_____

_____

_____

What is a story
about you that you
feel best captures
who you are?

What is something
about you that
other people might
find surprising?

_____

_____

_____

_____

What are you
most looking
forward to
today?

_____

_____

_____

_____

What is your passion?

_____

_____

_____

_____

What is the boldest thing you have ever done?

_____

_____

_____

_____

What is something kind
you are going to do for
someone else this week?

_____

_____

_____

_____

What is something you do
that makes the world a better
place? (It may be as simple
as smiling at strangers or
as complex as running your
own charity.)

_____

_____

_____

_____

What is your favorite
thing to do when
you get alone time?
(Yes, including that.)

_____

_____

_____

_____

Where is
your favorite
place to be?

_____

_____

_____

_____

What is something
you love seeing?
What makes your
world more beautiful?

Are you doing something that scares or challenges you right now? If so, what is it? If not, what is something that scares you that you would you like to do?

What is your favorite
guilty pleasure? (Choose
something that doesn't
harm yourself or others)

_____

_____

_____

_____

What is your favorite armor you put
on to face the world—an outfit you
wear that makes you feel great/
good-looking/smart/tough?

_____

_____

_____

_____

What leaves you
rejuvenated?

_____

_____

_____

_____

_____

What is
something lovely
you will do for
yourself today?

_____

_____

_____

_____

How would you most like to be described?

_____

_____

_____

_____

_____

_____

_____

_____

_____

_____

_____

What is the best
piece of advice you
can give someone
based on your life
experiences?

_____

_____

_____

_____

_____

_____

_____

_____

_____

CHAPTER 2

love

The most love I have ever felt came with the most physical pain I have ever experienced. Our daughter Vivienne ripped me open—both physically and spiritually—as she came into the world. It is an experience that isn't unique, and yet, it was the most special moment of my life. My wife, Cat, was holding one of my thighs as one of my best friends, McKerrin, held the other. My mother-in-law, Norma, was also there—and yes, it takes a *very* special woman to be the kind of mother-in-law you would allow to be present when you are straddling stirrups as a spotlight beams onto your brightly lit vagina. My other best friend, Alex, arrived straight from a film set just as Vivienne was born. Alex had a receptionist call up to the room and was greeted by a chorus of "*No*, now is *not* a good time to come up!" that she could hear through the receptionist's phone. Our OBGYN, Dr. Regina Edmond, caught Vivi, and a nurse placed her on my chest for skin-to-skin time. As Cat and I looked down at our precious, beloved little girl . . . Vivienne peed all over me. I've never been so happy.

This is the moment of *my* greatest love: the moment everything changed for me forever in the best way. That moment looks different for each of us. I want to acknowledge that this is not everyone's story. Not everybody wants to be a parent. Some people have lost children, spouses, or loved ones in childbirth. Some people have longed to have this experience and have not been able to do so. Many of us are mourning and grieving in so many ways. I want to fully honor and send love to everyone whose heart is aching. Life can be painful. Love can be painful.

The pain of love is part of this chapter too. When we talk about love, we usually focus on the bliss of it. That feeling is real, but pain is also a part of love. There is a saying: "Grief is the price of love."

I think that is almost correct. I believe grief *is* love. It's the resilient love that refuses to leave just because there is not a tangible place for it to go. It is love that lingers, at first ferociously, violently refusing to be ignored. Over time, grief becomes the love that gently reminds us of wonderful souls we still love and the things they shared with us—and, hopefully, we honor those souls by sharing that love with others and with ourselves.

This was true of my first boyfriend, Caleb. He was a sweet four-teen-year-old boy when we started dating. He was respectful, kind, and lovely. Our parents were friends. His younger brother, Ryan, was the boyfriend of my best friend at the time, ReAnna. Caleb took on the big emotional toll of having a girlfriend who had a terminally ill mother: He called me multiple times from school the day she died and had his mom drive him to meet me at ReAnna's house. Despite being just a kid himself, he handled having a grieving fourteen-year-old girlfriend so well.

Later, I had to be honest and break up with him. I loved him, but not the way I needed to in order to be his girlfriend. It would take me a few more years to realize I was a lesbian, but I already knew I didn't feel the way my friends did about boys. Caleb stayed my dear friend. After my stepfather remarried, the home became abusive, and my stepparents cut off my sisters and me from anyone who had previously been in our lives. Caleb and I had an inside joke about the characters Boris and Natasha from *Rocky and Bullwinkle* (if you are under thirty-five, you might have to look this one up), and he used the name "Boris" as an alter ego so that he could call and check on me. My stepmother thought the name was funny and would con-stantly laugh at this Boris guy from my new school. Caleb stayed my dear friend until his tragically early death at age thirty-one.

The love remains. I still have a little Boris figurine. I always will. Love is also wonderful, sexy, and fun! Don't worry, we're absolutely going there too. This chapter also covers Sex! Lust! Romance! Intense connection! My wife, Cat, proposed to me on our second date. Our first date was me flying her across four states for what was supposed to be a weekend booty-call, one-night-stand situation, but then she felt like home. What's a girl to do? I am here for a whirlwind romance.

I hope this chapter reminds you of all the love you have given and received. The people who have made you feel seen and understood and cherished. The people you adore, living and gone. I hope it reminds you of all the passion you've shared and enjoyed. I even hope it makes you blush just a little.

What is something
you could do today
that would show
someone else how
much you love them?

_____

_____

_____

_____

_____

_____

_____

_____

_____

What is your favorite
way someone has let
you know that they
love you?

Tell a story about
a person you
love dearly that
exemplifies why
you love them.

What is the best
pickup line anyone
has ever used on
you? Did it work?

_____

_____

_____

_____

Who was your
first love? Why
did you fall for
them?

_____

_____

_____

_____

Describe one of the most romantic experiences you've ever had.

_____

_____

_____

_____

_____

_____

_____

_____

_____

_____

Describe someone
you loved and lost. Tell
a story that would help
someone understand
the essence of who
they were.

Who is the
person who has
made you feel
the most loved?

_____

_____

_____

_____

What is your most
seductive trait?

_____

_____

_____

_____

_____

What is the most
adventurous sexual
activity you have
enjoyed trying?

What is something that
has made you swoon
that other people might
not find romantic?

Who is the person you love the most?

What is something
you love about
yourself?

What makes
you feel sexy?

What is the most
romantic thing you
have ever done for
someone else?

Who is someone
you have a deep,
platonic love for?

Describe a time
you felt loved
as a child.

_____

_____

_____

_____

Describe a time
you felt loved as
an adult.

_____

_____

_____

_____

Describe a time someone made you feel nurtured and comfortable.

What is an object that reminds you of someone you love?

_____

_____

_____

_____

_____

_____

_____

_____

_____

What is something
you could do
today to show
love to yourself?

What is the biggest
sacrifice a person has
made for you?

_____

_____

_____

_____

_____

What is the
biggest sacrifice
you have made for
someone else?

_____

_____

_____

_____

Have you ever rekindled a relationship or friendship after losing touch, fighting, or splitting up? What brought you back together?

Who is someone you
feel a lot of warmth
toward but don't
personally know?

_____

_____

_____

_____

Who is someone you
care deeply about
but only interact
with online?

_____

_____

_____

_____

Who is the first person you want to share news (good or bad) with?

_____

_____

_____

_____

Who is a person who seems genuinely delighted by your triumphs?

_____

_____

_____

_____

CHAPTER 3

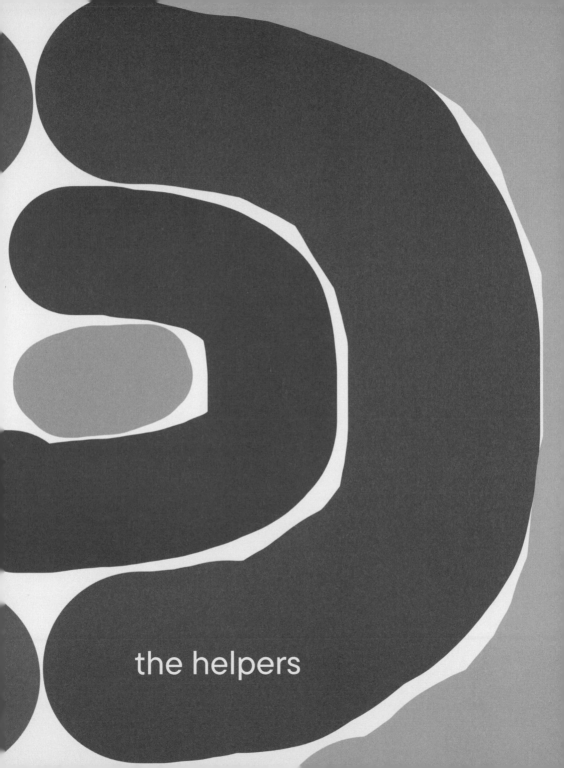

the helpers

I was eleven years old, sobbing in a sweltering central Florida hospital parking lot. The van didn't have AC and my stepfather hadn't left me the key anyway, so, with my two younger sisters sleeping in the back seat, I had flung the back doors wide open in an attempt to help the humid air circulate. That's when she saw me. She had slipped out of the hospital waiting area to smoke a cigarette. Her leathery skin was glistening with sweat in the midday heat when she noticed me and called me over to her. Being a responsible preteen left in charge of my two younger sisters while my stepfather rushed my mother into the ER, I reacted . . . well, more like a terrified kid whose mommy was seriously and mysteriously ill. I went immediately to the stranger. She took a drag on the cigarette in her right hand and scooped me into a hug with her left hand. She asked what was wrong. Dutifully keeping my eyes on the brown-and-tan van doors in case my sisters stirred, I told her my mom had gotten ill . . . again. Her migraines were getting worse, and after she'd started uncontrollably vomiting in pain during our two-hour drive home from a weekend family trip, she had begged to go to the emergency room. No one knew what was wrong, and we were scared. (We'd later find out that it was cancer.) The stranger listened and told me that she was worried about someone inside the hospital too. We sat together for a while, then she went inside, and I went back to the van, feeling less alone. I don't know her name, and I never saw her again.

Why did I tell you a story about little Mandy ignoring stranger danger and gulping down secondhand smoke? Because spiritual connection doesn't always come in perfect packaging. We all have ephemeral guides: strangers who come into our lives for only a moment, but it ends up being the *right* moment. We can also be that person for others. You don't have to achieve a certain amount of enlightenment to give a stranger the smile that saves their life. You've done it already. I promise you.

Of course, it's not just strangers who change our lives. We have friends, parents, grandparents, guardians, teachers, and coworkers who have all been the perfect person for some moment. When I was in eighth grade, my mother died of the same cancer that had brought her to the ER when I was eleven. I felt so lost and confused that I went to school the very next day. I didn't know what else to do in a world without my mom. I tried to just keep going—to keep making straight As, teaching Sunday school, cheerleading, being a good big sister—but inside, my world had shattered. I couldn't even comprehend my own grief, much less share it with anyone else. So I didn't. My mother died on February 6, 1997. On March 6, 1997, my science teacher, Ms. Wells, walked into my English classroom and said she needed to take me out of class. My English teacher nodded, and I followed Ms. Wells, confused. We walked off campus to the lake across the street (in central Florida, there is an alligator-filled lake across any given street). She sat down on top of a picnic table with her feet on the bench in front of us. I joined her and we looked out at the lake. She pulled out a carton of strawberries. "I know you haven't said anything, but I wanted you to know that someone remembered that it is the one-month anniversary of your mother's death."

It's been over twenty years since that happened and it still makes me tear up. To have felt so seen, and to have been so simply comforted, meant so much. These are the kinds of moments in life that show us the best in humanity. I want to take this month to celebrate that. Each day, you will answer one question about the people who have made *your* life beautiful: the people who are still with you, those who are gone, and those ephemeral guides whose presence in your life was fleeting but impactful. As Mr. Rogers's mother so famously instructed: "Look for the helpers."

Who is a person who
made you feel safe,
seen, or cared for, even
briefly, as a child?

How did you
meet your
best friend?

Write about a time someone believed in you so much that it changed how you felt about yourself.

What is something
kind a stranger has
done for you?

_____

_____

_____

_____

_____

Describe a time
someone was there
for you during a
scary moment.

_____

_____

_____

_____

Who is
someone who
has advocated
for you?

_____

_____

_____

_____

Who is a person you're glad
exists/existed? (You don't
have to have met, but it
must be someone who has
changed your life.)

_____

_____

_____

_____

Tell a story
about a kind
thing someone
did for you.

Who is someone you'd like
to thank for something, big
or small, but haven't?
(If they're still around, you
get bonus points if you take
today to thank them.)

Has getting to know a person
ever dramatically changed your
perspective on something?

Has a stranger ever given you
a random compliment that
made your day/week/month or
helped you get over a slump?

Who is someone
who shares a
passion with you?

What's something
nice someone said or
did for you this week?

_____

_____

_____

_____

Who is a person
who encourages
you to be the best
version of yourself?

_____

_____

_____

_____

Who is a person you
mistrusted at first who
later proved you wrong?

What is a gift someone
gave you that made
you feel especially
seen or understood?

Write about a
person you met
and had an instant
connection with.

Who is someone who
has touched your life
even though you've
never actually met?

_____

_____

_____

_____

Who is a singer or
musician whose
work speaks to
your soul?

_____

_____

_____

_____

What author's writing resonates with you on a personal level? Why?

Who is a person you can speak with and always leave feeling better about yourself?

Who is someone in
your personal life
you admire?

Who is a historical
figure you admire?
Why? How are you
like them?

Describe a
time someone
mentored you.

Who is a
person who
admires you?

_____

_____

_____

_____

_____

Who is a person who has
encouraged you to leave
your comfort zone in a
positive way?

_____

_____

_____

_____

Who is a person you have
mentored or helped?
What did you get out of
the experience?

Have you ever given a
stranger a compliment
and watched the way it
impacted them? How did
you feel afterward?

Write about a person
who gave you a
boost just when you
needed it most.

Who is someone
who makes
you laugh?

_____

_____

_____

_____

Who is the person
you feel like your
best self around?

_____

_____

_____

_____

CHAPTER 4

the trailblazers

I went on a road trip with my grandparents when I was in my late teens. I had just gotten into a relationship with my first real girlfriend, and I was very, very much in the closet. While we were traveling, we went to stay with some of my grandparents' Marine Corps buddies at a farm in upstate New York. One friend, who was a colonel, had a sister in her late eighties who was also visiting. She and I sat on the porch, and she told me stories of how she had traveled cross country as a young opera singer with nothing but sheet music in her car at a time when women didn't often travel alone. She had harrowing and thrilling adventures, and she met and fell in love with a few women along the way. I was awestruck. I had never met an elderly lesbian before, and it was a revelation to me. Here was a woman who had lived her life authentically during a time I couldn't even imagine. I came out to her during a long walk along the perimeter of the farm. I also told her I was afraid to tell my very conservative grandparents. She listened, and I felt so relieved to talk with someone who understood. When we got back to the farmhouse, she went to the piano and played "Somewhere Over the Rainbow" as a private message between us.

This moment has stayed with me throughout my life. It gave me courage, and when I did finally come out a few months later, I thought of her. I also thought of her when I packed up and moved cross-country from North Carolina to Los Angeles to pursue my own dreams. That one brief weekend with this stranger was life-changing and impactful. I will always carry her story with me. If that brave young woman could pursue her dreams of working in the arts and could love women openly and authentically at a time when it was even less societally acceptable than now, there is no excuse for me to not fully live my own life. I owe it to myself, to her, and to those like her who worked so hard and so bravely.

There have been trailblazers—people we have known intimately, and those we've only "met" through their art and literature—in all of our lives. This chapter celebrates those who came before us, helped to shape our world, and inspired us to stay true to ourselves in difficult times.

Write about a time you heard about another person's experiences and it gave you an aha moment about yourself.

Who is a person in history
who paved the way for
you in some way?

_____

_____

_____

_____

Who is a person you
know personally who
paved the way for
you in some way?

_____

_____

_____

_____

What is a song that speaks or has spoken to you on a deep level that has helped you better understand something about yourself?

_____

_____

_____

_____

Who is a trailblazer you admire? In what way are you like them?

_____

_____

_____

_____

Write about a time someone invested in you in a way that changed your life.

_____

_____

_____

_____

What is a film or television show that helped you realize something about yourself?

_____

_____

_____

_____

Write about a time
that you were
first exposed to
something new and
immediately knew
"this is me."

Who is a fictional
character who helped
you see an authentic
part of yourself?

Write about a time
you learned from
someone else's
negative example.

Write about a time you
learned from someone's
positive example.

_____

_____

_____

_____

_____

What is a book you've
read that taught you
something new about
yourself?

_____

_____

_____

_____

Who is someone
you wanted to be
like as a child?

Who is someone
you would
like to be more
like now?

What is your favorite
quote from a person
in history?

Write about a time that
someone pointed out
something about you
that you'd never noticed
until they said it.

If you could interview
one person, living
or dead, and learn from
them, who would it be?

_____

_____

_____

_____

In what ways do
you feel like a
trailblazer?

_____

_____

_____

_____

Write about a
moment you felt
truly seen and
understood by
someone else.

What is something
that changed the
trajectory of your
family's history?

What is your favorite work of art by a visual artist? Why does it speak to you?

Write about a time you witnessed someone standing up for something they believed in.

Write about a time
someone did something
brave and inspired you to
be brave in turn.

_____

_____

_____

_____

_____

In what ways
do you inspire
others?

_____

_____

_____

_____

Write about the
most resourceful
person you know.

Who is a person in your
life who has overcome
great adversity?

Who is a person who
gave you an opportunity
or opened a door for you?

Whom have you
opened doors for?
What did that experience
mean to you?

What is something kind you can do to let a person who opened a door for you know how much they mean to you?

_____

_____

_____

_____

One day you will be an ancestor. What do you hope your memory will inspire in future generations?

_____

_____

_____

_____

CHAPTER 5

the
little
things

I don't believe in little things. I used to think that there was such a thing as something small or insignificant, but after years of life (and therapy), I've come to a different belief about the "little things": a friend who brings you a chocolate bar on a rough day, someone remembering what you're interested in, a warm smile from a stranger in the moment you need it the most, a hug from someone you love. These "little things" are the things that make life—not that make life worth living, but that *make life*. Real connection, however brief, is being truly seen by another person while you really see them. That is everything. It's the meaning of life. Yes, here it is in Chapter 5 of a guided journal: connection. Our souls are meant to touch one another. We're supposed to be connected, to be part of each other. Figuring out how to do that is everything.

I believe those moments can be as simple as when my friend Kendra brought me a can of sparkling water at preschool pickup because she knew I had had a difficult morning. Or when Kate forced me to come to her house for dinner after we'd had a scary house fire and she knew I had no business cooking. When Jennifer volunteered to watch my daughter so my wife could get work done while I traveled cross-country to attend my aunt's funeral. It's also me traveling cross-country to be there with my cousins as their mother was buried. It's my wife getting me yellow roses every year on the anniversary of my mother's death, and me getting her the plants and food she loves on her father's birthday and the anniversary of his death. It's forming a pod with Jared and Jeffrey through a pandemic so our kids could each have a playmate and we could have adult interaction. It's my friends Jen and Caroline sitting at a hospital all day with me through a rape kit, and it's having someone calling to check in, and a very literal touchstone to hold, as I waited for the results. It's the not-so-tiny ways my soul sisters Alex and McKerrin have shown up for me so many times I wouldn't even be able to write them all out.

It's even the pieces of art, films, or books that speak to us and let us know we aren't alone in the ways we experience the world. It's also the connection you have to yourself and the favorite quiet spaces you create.

Let's celebrate all the not-so-little things that shape our lives.

What is a gift someone
has given you that means
the world to you?

_____

_____

_____

_____

What is an inside joke
you have a with a friend
that never fails to make
you smile?

_____

_____

_____

_____

Write about a time someone cooked or purchased a favorite meal for you.

What is something
someone has done
for you during a hard
time that meant a lot?

Where is a
place you feel
serene?

Write about a
time someone
cared for you
while you were ill.

What is a piece of art
in your home that has
significance to you?

_____

_____

_____

_____

_____

What is something
you do that makes
you feel connected
to your body?

_____

_____

_____

_____

_____

Write about a time
someone took
you somewhere
because they knew
you would love it.

What is a "random,"
"weird," or "unusual"
object that means a
lot to you?

Write about a time someone complimented you in a "small" way, but it meant a lot to you.

What is a song that you
associate with something
deeply personal?

_____

_____

_____

_____

Where is your
favorite place in
the world?

_____

_____

_____

_____

What is a piece of
clothing someone
gave you that
you love?

_____

_____

_____

_____

Is there an animal that
brings joy to your life?
Describe them.

_____

_____

_____

_____

_____

Where is your
favorite space in
your home?

_____

_____

_____

_____

_____

What is a fun or silly
tradition you have
with someone?

_____

_____

_____

_____

_____

What is something
"small" you could do
today that would make
the day a bit better?

_____

_____

_____

_____

What is something
"small" you could do for
someone else today to
make their day better?

_____

_____

_____

_____

What is something that you found touching or helpful after a loss?

What's a treat that instantly brings you back to a beloved memory?

Write about an
email, tweet, DM,
letter, or message
someone sent
you that means a
lot to you.

Describe something
you cherish that once
belonged to a loved one.

Where do you
most want to
be when you
feel down?

What is an accessory that
makes you feel good,
strong, empowered, or
cool when you wear it?

_____

_____

_____

_____

What is a smell
that brings you
comfort?

_____

_____

_____

_____

Write about a time
someone lent you
something and it
helped you out.

Write about a time
someone participated in
an event or activity just
because you love it.

What is something
that you love to
do for fun?

Who is the most
recent person to
make you laugh?
What was so funny?

What will you do today to bring a tiny (but powerful) spark of joy to someone else's life?

CHAPTER 6

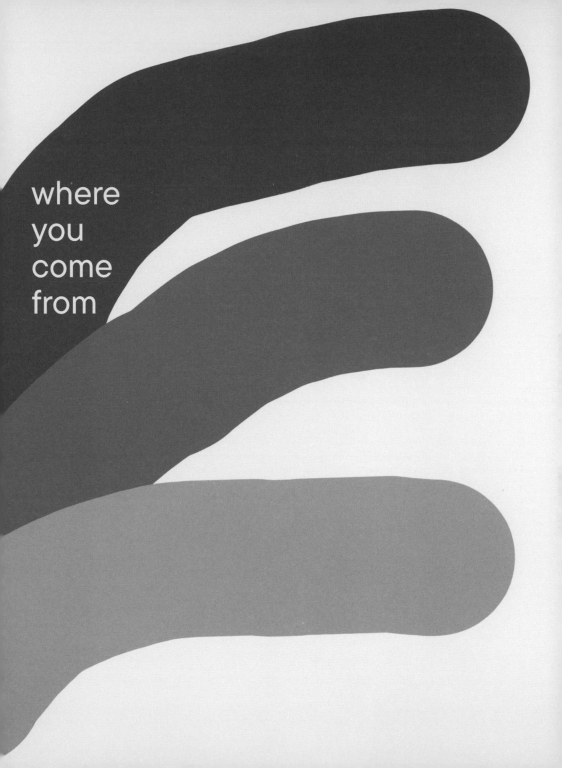

where
you
come
from

I am a "Shawshank baby." At least, that's the joking nickname I gave myself after I learned a little about the way I came to exist.

For many years, when I asked my mother about my biological father, she would give me contradictory or convoluted stories. Finally, when I was in my early twenties and had just moved to Los Angeles—and after my mother had already passed—I discovered the truth thanks to my excellent Google skills, bits of information my mother had given me, and online prison records. Here's the true story, to the best of my knowledge: When my mother was a young art major, she answered an ad in her college newspaper and started a pen pal relationship with a prison inmate. Eventually their letters turned amorous, and she went to meet him during visiting hours. He did what any lovestruck inmate would do next: He broke out of prison and, instead of skipping town, went to find my mother. During the six-month period that he was on the lam, I was conceived. Then he was recaptured, and my mom wanted nothing to do with him. She got rid of every letter and photo so that little Amanda grew up with no contact with her father and no clue who he was.

I never met my father. He died in 2006, just a few months before I was able to piece together this story and the details of who he was and where he'd lived. I thought that was the end of things, and it was—until 2019, thanks to an unrelated viral tweet about my mom's side of the family.

Every December 7th, I share a story about my mom's grandparents, my great-grandparents, who were stationed at Pearl Harbor with their three young sons. Their youngest child at the time was my grandfather. On the morning of the attacks, my great-grandfather saw the planes flying low toward them and realized what was happening. He instructed his sons to smile and wave at the pilots as they passed over them. My great-uncle Harold swore that a pilot saw them wave and then turned his plane in another direction. Great-Granddaddy Deibert had to join the rest of the Marines protecting the base, which meant that Granny, my great-grandmother, was left to look after three little boys during a bombing. She climbed on top of the toilet to look out of the bathroom window, saw a submarine sink, and knew they were not safe. So she went into full "mom mode." She grabbed her sons' Christmas presents, three toy pop guns, from under her bed. Then she took her boys into the jungle to hide. There, Granny crouched down with her young sons, who pretended to shoot down the planes firing real bullets at them. My grandfather, who was six at the time, still has some shrapnel from that day. He has told me many stories about the attack and the aftermath—it made for one hell of a show-and-tell in history class!—and I have the family legacy of a fierce mother who did what she had to do to protect her children.

As I said, I share that story every year, but in 2019 it led to a whole new family revelation. A man in Canada read it and emailed me to see if I was related to his branch of the Deibert family. I logged on to my long-forgotten Ancestry account to check—and I got the surprise of my life. I had no answers for this stranger, but someone had updated and added to the very little information I'd learned about my father's side of the family many years before. It now included names and marriage certificates of his sisters. One of them, my aunt Jane, had passed away. Two others were still alive, and they were on Facebook! Let me tell you, it is incredibly awkward to send strangers a Facebook message that says, "Hi! I think I might be your niece." Luckily for me, I apparently come from kind and welcoming people. We exchanged a few messages and pieced together some things, and my brand-new aunt Joyce gave me something I'd never had before: a photo of my father. It was startling to see so much of my own face stare back at me. I don't know why I hadn't really expected to look like him. Later, in 2021, I met my aunt Joyce in person and had the surreal experience of going through family photos with her. She locked her piercing blue eyes on mine and asked, "Did your mom have blue eyes?"

"No," I said. "No one on my mom's side of the family did." And then we sat and smiled in silence, staring at each other with our matching eyes.

This story is a small part of my journey to learn more about who I am and where I come from. The experiences of those who raised us, those who loved us, and even those who wronged us are all woven into our own stories.

Let's get into yours now. As you answer this chapter's questions, feel free to write about your family of origin or the family of your heart.

What is a cool
bit of family
history you
know?

What childhood traditions do you carry on?

What is something
you didn't know was
"unusual" about your
upbringing until later?

What is something
you admire about
one of your relatives?

What did your parents or
guardians do for a living?
What do you do?

What is a recipe or meal
that has huge significance
to you? Why?

Tell a story about
an amazing woman
in your family.

Who is a man in your
family whom you look up
to in some way?

_____

_____

_____

_____

What is something
about your family
that makes you
feel proud?

_____

_____

_____

Write about a
time you revealed
something about
yourself to your family
and it went well.

How did you end
up with the name
you have?

_____

_____

_____

_____

_____

What smell do you
associate with someone
who cared for you when
you were young?

_____

_____

_____

_____

What is something
kind that a relative or
caretaker did for you?

_____

_____

_____

_____

_____

What is something
kind that you did
for a relative?

_____

_____

_____

_____

_____

What is something you are proud your family overcame?

What does
your last
name mean?

Describe a way you are
proud to differ from
your own upbringing.

If you could go back
in time and meet a
relative you never
got to know, who
would it be?

_____

_____

_____

_____

What is something
about your upbringing
that would surprise
other people?

_____

_____

_____

_____

What was
your favorite
childhood toy?

Do you have an old family
photo from before your
time that you love? What
do you love about it?

What is a trait you like about yourself that you got from someone who was influential in your childhood?

_____

_____

_____

Who introduced you to your current passions?

_____

_____

_____

_____

What is a bit of family history you have worked to overcome?

What is your
favorite thing about
your heritage?

_____

_____

_____

_____

What was your
favorite way to spend
a day as a child?

_____

_____

_____

_____

Write a letter to one
person in your family
thanking them for
something.

Have you ever been
surprised to discover
something about your
family? If so, what was it?

Who is someone
in your family who
makes you feel good
about yourself?

What are your dreams for your own family—the family that you have created or want to create? (This doesn't necessarily include a spouse or children, if that is not your desire.)

change is scary.
you are brave.

You are amazing. As is. Right now. We've been in this together for six chapters now. Hopefully by this point you've looked at your answers about all the things you've survived and all the people you've loved, and it's helped you to realize just *how* amazing you are. You've done incredible things. You have been strong and brave, you have taken bold risks, and you have loved and lost and laughed.

There are also things you still want to do. Some of those are things you haven't been able to do because of wildly unfair circumstances that have happened to you. These are the situations you cannot control, and you have worked hard to thrive despite them. There are also things you've been putting off. And *then* there are the lies: absolute untruths you have been taught and told to internalize, and that you have *believed*, about why you could never do something you want to do. Those are the most difficult, and most important, things to unravel, and we're going to take them on together. Sure, some things just suck. Some things aren't fair. I'm not talking about those things. This chapter is about new beginnings and about letting go of the things that are holding you back.

This chapter might be a little frightening, but we've already established that you have been through scarier. The very best things that have ever happened to me came from wild leaps of faith. (Not *reckless* leaps—I am a realist who loves preparation.) I moved to Los Angeles with nothing. My then-girlfriend and I couldn't afford a moving truck to take from North Carolina to LA. So I took a leap of faith that eventually something would work out, and I gave away all my furniture: a beautiful antique desk I had spent hours sanding, staining, and restoring; a sofa I had reupholstered with my grandfather; and a bookshelf that we built. I gave away everything but the throw pillows my grandma and I had sewn together. I found a woman on Craigslist whose daughter was pregnant and had moved back home from California with nothing. It felt like kismet to give this new mom all my stuff as I headed to California myself. It also felt nice to know that I was helping her with free furniture.

I left in a caravan with my then-girlfriend, plus my ex-girlfriend, and all of our cats. (Yes, that's me moving with a girlfriend AND an ex... I'm a lesbian stereotype.) When we arrived in LA, those throw pillows were all we had for furniture. No jobs, no money—just a very small apartment in Sherman Oaks and a lot of small pillows on the living-room floor. We were friendly and got to know our neighbors a bit. A week later, one of the downstairs neighbors lost her brother. He left her his home and all his furniture. She, in turn, gave us all the furniture she had in her apartment: chairs, a pull-out sofa, and all the things we needed to survive. It felt like such a wild full-circle moment. Less than a month after I'd given away all my furniture, I was in a fully furnished apartment again. I'm so sorry her brother died. I'm so grateful she shared his generosity with us.

I've taken other leaps of faith throughout my life: like using all the money I had saved to study abroad when I was in college or many years later, using money from a severance package to get pregnant even though my wife Cat and I had no idea if or when I would have another job. It was the best decision of my entire life.

Even creating this journal came from me having to let go of things I believed for way too long: that I am "too much" and that I need to make myself smaller. I had to adjust and realize that people truly do want to connect . . . even with me. One of the most difficult things in the world for me is believing I am worthy. If this is your struggle too, please know that you aren't alone. It's so incredibly difficult for those of us who received negative messages as a child or grew up with abuse, neglect, or bullying.

Maybe the lie you cuddle up with at night looks or sounds a little different. Whatever it is, let's get it out of your way, okay? Get ready for an adventure.

"Future you" deserves so much love. What is something you can do right now as a gift to your future self?

_____

_____

_____

_____

What is something you are glad you did before you were old enough to "know better"?

_____

_____

_____

_____

Write about a time you questioned something you'd previously accepted as truth, or the way things are, and it led to an epiphany—one of those mind-shifting moments.

Take a few moments to really think about where you are—emotionally, physically, mentally, and so on—right now. Are there routines and patterns that you've accidentally formed and that you would like to change? Write about one thing you could switch up.

What is something you'd like to change about the way you dress or style yourself? Is there a hairstyle or accessory you've always wanted to try but haven't?

What is something you wish you made more time for? How can you arrange your schedule in a way that could help make it fit better?

What is something you've
been afraid to try, but
would like to?

Stop and do something you've been
putting off that is possible to do
right now. (Yes, right now!) Come
back and write about how you feel
about it after you've done it.

What is something that helps motivate you when you feel stuck? (It may be as simple as a piece of art, a quote, a walk, or a shower.)

What would you most like to be known for?

What is a positive habit
you would like to develop?
Start it today, if possible.

_____

_____

_____

_____

_____

What is something that
makes you feel fantastic
after you've done it?

_____

_____

_____

_____

_____

Think back to who you were five years ago. Is there something you wish that version of you had done to help set you up now? What can you do now to help the version of you who's five years in the future?

What are you extremely
good at? What are your
special gifts?

_____

_____

_____

_____

_____

Who is someone you
would like to spend
more time with?

_____

_____

_____

_____

_____

What is the best part of your day?

What can you do today to take extra care of your physical body?

What can you do today
to take extra care of your
mental health?

_____

_____

_____

_____

_____

What can you do
today to stimulate
your mind?

_____

_____

_____

_____

_____

What can you do today to help fulfill yourself on a spiritual level? If the word "spiritual" doesn't resonate with you, what can you do today to center yourself?

What is something
you wish more people
noticed about you?

Who is someone in your
life you would like to get
to know better?

Who is a fictional character you would love to be seen as similar to? What is it about them you admire? In what ways are you similar already?

What is something you can do to creatively refuel yourself this week? (Yes, even if you don't consider yourself "a creative.")

What is a compliment you would love to receive?

Do you have a bad habit you'd like to break? What is it? Why do you think you do it? (When I am stressed, I pick my cuticles until they bleed. You don't need to know this, but I don't want you to feel alone or judged.)

What is
something that
excites you?

What is something
stressful in your life that
you could let go of and
not cause any harm?

What is something
you would like to
change about your
home environment?

What is one small change to your ambiance that you can make right now? (Yes, just a little thing to make where you are in this moment a tiny bit more pleasant.)

What is something
you tried this month
that you would like
to keep doing?
What did you learn
about yourself?

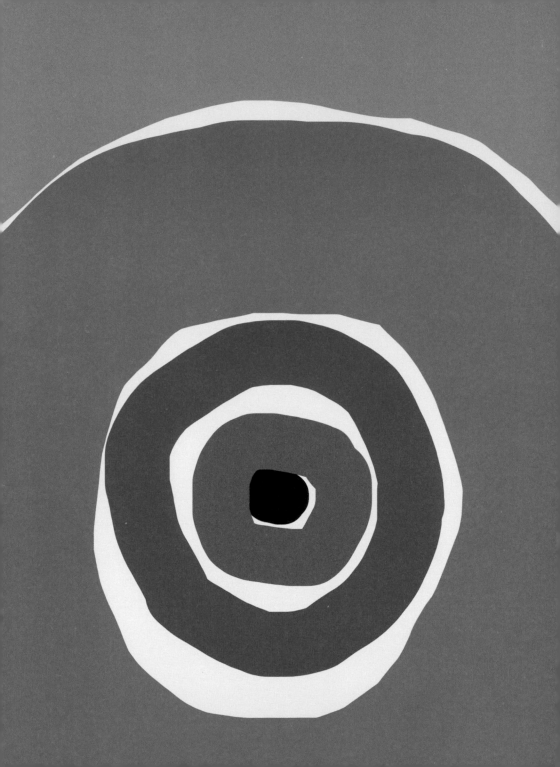

CHAPTER 8

the
things
we
rarely
share

I was in Paris at the base of the Eiffel Tower with former Vice President Al Gore, Kofi Annan (the seventh secretary-general of the United Nations), several Obama Administration advisors, multiple international political leaders and Duran Duran on the day of the horrific and tragic November 2015 attacks in Paris by ISIS. Yes, that's a lot to take in on so many levels.

This was my first international trip away from my daughter, who was then ten months old and at home with my wife Cat. It was my first year working as a writer for former Vice President Gore's *24 Hours of Reality*, an annual broadcast full of world leaders, scientists, activists, celebrities, and musical guests spotlighting the global effects of the climate crisis and various nations' responses and progress. It is a project I had the privilege of working on for four years, and it is one of the things I am most proud of professionally. In 2015, we were in Paris just before the adoption of the monumental Paris Agreement.

We were live on air when the attacks began. There were sirens everywhere. Paris was in chaos. We kept getting news: first one shooting, and then the next—more tragedy, more horror. It was gut-wrenching to be with our French crew members as they tried to contact and check on relatives, loved ones, and friends. It was also scary and disorienting. I was still breastfeeding at the time and had been pumping and dumping to keep my milk supply up while I was away from my baby for the week. At some point, my chest became so painfully engorged that I had to run across the field to the restroom to pump and get relief. The next few days were a mix of intensely sad and beautiful interactions with Parisians. I will always remember the way they went about their lives, sharing food, drink, and stories. A French woman even interpreted the news for me so I would know what was happening.

The full story is much more complex than what I am writing here. It's for a whole different kind of book. My point in sharing this

part of the story is to show that we have all had extreme experiences. Some of our stories are sad, wild, or profound, and they don't
always come up in day-to-day conversations. For example, I recently
realized that many of my good friends didn't know this story because
it happened before our kids attended school together, so when I
casually referred to it at a playdate, they all stared at me with their
jaws dropped. Some of our stories don't come up because they are
difficult to share. I don't often tell people that I am a survivor of years
of childhood sexual abuse. For a long time, that had a lot to do with
my own feelings of guilt and shame around circumstances that were
not my fault. It took many years, and therapy, to get to a place where
I realize that it is not my shame to carry .

We don't always want to share what we've been through,
and we don't have to. I want to be very clear about the difference
between *secrets* and *privacy*. We all have a right to privacy. Privacy
is good. You get to choose where, when, and *if* you want to share
your story. No one is owed it. *Ever*. But if you feel like you can't share
something because of feelings of shame—if it feels like a *secret*—I
urge you to talk with someone you trust who can try to help you work
through that. Whatever you've been through is unique to you; at the
same time, you are not alone. Many of us have so much more we've
experienced and endured than people know, and sometimes those
moments of "me too" can mean the world.

So here is a private place to cultivate some of those moments,
both good and bad, that we don't always have the space or opportunity to talk about. Don't worry: Not every question in this chapter
will be probing into difficult memories. This is for your interesting
tidbits and fun facts too! This is everything you don't get to talk
about nearly enough. It's about life. *Your* life. You deserve to honor
the things you've experienced. Whether or not you share it, and who
you share it with, is entirely up to you.

What is the most
dangerous thing you
have survived?

_____

_____

_____

_____

_____

What would you
say is the most
adventurous thing
you have done?

_____

_____

_____

_____

What is a moment that changed your life forever?

What is something that
has happened to you that
you would classify as a
supernatural encounter?

_____

_____

_____

_____

What is the
strangest
job you've
ever had?

_____

_____

_____

_____

Write about a time
you were given a
second chance at
something.

What is the wildest
or riskiest thing
you've ever done
that turned out well?

What is something difficult you have overcome?

What is the best
thing that has
ever happened
to you?

What is the bravest thing you have ever done?

_____

_____

_____

_____

_____

What is something unique about your life now?

_____

_____

_____

_____

_____

What is something
you've done that still
makes you laugh when
you think about it?

What is the most
unusual living situation
you've ever had?

Who is a person you were shocked, surprised, or delighted to meet? Why was meeting them so stunning?

What is something that happened to you that caught you completely off guard in a good way?

Write about something
you experienced,
something that was truly
scary at the time, but
that ultimately turned
out to be okay.

Imagine hearing the story of something difficult you have experienced told by someone else. What words of love, support, and encouragement would you give to that person who has been through so much?

What is something you
would like to share with
others but have a difficult
time opening up about?

_____

_____

_____

_____

Who is someone you
went through a difficult
experience with? What was
it like to have them there?

_____

_____

_____

_____

_____

What is the best
surprise anyone has
ever given you?

What is the most
fun thing you have
ever done?

What is a story
from your life that
amazes people
when they hear it?

What is a subject you
know a tremendous
amount about?

_____

_____

_____

_____

_____

What is something
you are extremely
good at?

_____

_____

_____

_____

_____

What's the boldest
fashion risk you've
ever taken?

What's the most
unusual thing you've
ever purchased?

What is something people
would be surprised to hear
you have never done?

When have you
most impressed
someone else?

What is an
accomplishment
you are proud to
have achieved?

What is something
you've done that has
helped to heal you in
some way?

What's your
absolute favorite
story to tell?

CHAPTER 9

when
things
are
dark

I spent the night before my mother's funeral in the guest bedroom of my grandparents' next-door neighbors' house with my mom's best friend, "Aunt" Janice. We'd traveled from our home in Florida to North Carolina, where my grandparents lived and where Mom would be buried. The people who ran the morgue were family friends, and they drove Mom's body in a hearse across the four states. It was a morbid and sad road trip, and I spent the entire time staring at a bouquet of sunflowers that my school friends and teachers had sent me, which my family allowed me to bring on our journey. When we arrived, there weren't enough rooms in my grandparents' house to hold us all so Aunt Janice and I ended up next door. We were sad, and as we laid there in the dark, we started talking about my mom and telling stories. The next thing I knew, we were having a giggling and laughing fit. It was the first time I'd really, truly laughed since my mom died the week before. I always wondered if the neighbors we were staying with, Ms. Elva and Mr. George, heard our laughter and thought it was weird.

I wasn't happy. I was the saddest I'd ever been in my life, but I also felt loved and understood. Aunt Janice didn't try to cheer me up. She didn't say all the things that people had been saying all week that made me want to scream. You know the ones I mean: "Everything happens for a reason." "She's in a better place." No. The best place to be for a thirty-five-year-old mother of three little girls is with her babies. Spouting platitudes and trying to simply cheer someone up is never the answer. It just isn't. The best thing to do with a person who is hurting is to acknowledge their pain. Be there with them. Say, "This sucks. I'm sorry." I was able to laugh with Aunt Janice because she was also able to hurt with me. The laughter and the pain came together. It might not have made sense on paper, but it makes all the sense in the world to people who are grieving. The only way through our pain is *through* it. Not hiding from it. This is true when tragedy strikes, and it is true when life throws shitty things like depression at you. What you don't need is a meme about how you should just go exercise or smile more. Would a walk be helpful? Eh, probably, but when you don't feel up to leaving the house, having someone shame you for not doing it sure isn't going to make things better.

This is the chapter for when things are hard. Really, truly hard. We're going to talk about the things that help you process grief and combat the lies your minds might tell you. I hope that when you go through something difficult—as you have done before and might be doing right now—you can revisit this chapter and your answers for reminders that you know how to be there for yourself and that you are not alone. You might not be able to see me or feel me, but please know that I want to be there holding your hand through this.

What is something someone
did for you during a rough
time that made you feel
loved or supported?

Write about a time you connected with someone else over a shared sorrow, loss, or suffering. How did that connection feel?

Is there a film, TV
show, or book that
brings you comfort?

Where is the
coziest spot in
your home?

Do you have a go-to ritual or tradition that helps you acknowledge and process grief or tragedy? If not, what would you like one to look like for you?

What is something you can do today to honor and acknowledge your feelings with kindness toward yourself?

What is your gift—
something you are
good at that makes the
world a better place?

_____

_____

_____

_____

What is something
someone has said to you
while you were hurting
or grieving that was
actually helpful?

_____

_____

_____

_____

What is something you wish no one would ever say to you again? What do you wish they'd say instead?

What song do you like
to listen to when you
are feeling sad?

What advice would you
offer someone going
through something
difficult that you have
been through or are
going through?

What is a book, film, piece of art, pop culture reference, or meme that has shown you that other people have been through something similar to your own struggles and experiences? What has made you feel seen?

What clothing
do you feel most
comforted in?

Who is the most unexpected
person who reached out to
you during a hard time? What
did it mean to you?

What is something that
serves as a touchstone to
remind you of something
you like about yourself?

Write about a time
someone really
listened to you.

Describe
your favorite
outdoor spot.

What is a way you
move your body that
feels good to you?

What is a food or beverage that brings you comfort?

What is a scent that fills you with lovely memories?

Who is someone
you love deeply?
Describe what you
love about them.

What is something
that brings you
pleasure?

Write about a time
you brought comfort
to someone else.

What is something pleasant you could do today that is outside of your normal routine?

How can you
show yourself
compassion
today?

_____

_____

_____

_____

What is something on
your to-do list that you
could reasonably give
up in order to make
space for self-care?

_____

_____

_____

_____

When do you feel
most connected
to yourself?

What is something
you can do today to
nurture your body?

What is something you can do today to honor the people in your life that you have lost?

What is something you like about your current surroundings?

CHAPTER 10

to help
you
change
the
world

Our last family vacation before my mother passed was paid for by her hospice nurses. These kind women took up an office collection and sent us to Disney World, where we stayed in an accessible hotel room to accommodate Mom's wheelchair and need for rest. Our grandmother, Memommie, went with us as well. It's a bittersweet, but mostly sweet, memory. Mom got to watch her girls have fun and do something almost normal. I'll never forget how kind those nurses were and how much they saw not only my mother's pain, but also the suffering that her three little girls were going through. It made me want to be that kind of person: someone who sees others' pain and wants to do whatever I can to make their lives better, even in the times in my life when I haven't had much to give.

Several years ago, I sat on the floor by my sleeping daughter's toddler bed and sobbed when I read about children being taken from their parents at the US-Mexico border. I wasn't the only mother moved to action. Acquaintances of mine started the organization Immigrant Families Together, which at first was not even an organization, but rather a network of people—mostly moms—who wanted to help. They raised money to help pay bail for parents being held and then set up WhatsApp conversations to create a trail of people who could drive these parents to their children, who were sometimes being held on the other side of the country. I asked how I could help. I drafted a few letters and helped with some social media, but I learned that the biggest way I could contribute was through my Twitter platform. I started posting links to fundraise for mothers' bail funds one at a time. We raised a $15,000 bail fund and got a mom out and on the way to her child within eight hours. Then we helped pay bail for another mother . . . and another. Through WhatsApp, I was able to privately see the photos and videos of the mothers and children reunited. It broke my heart and restored my spirit all at once. I only played a tiny role, and yet, I was able to help—to use my resources and do *something*. Right now, I am helping Miry's List outfit recently arrived Afghan refugee children with warm winter clothes. I did seven charity runs for St. Jude's in 2021. These are not big things, but they remind me that I can do a lot just on my own.

If all of us do a little, we make a huge difference. We can help each other be an avalanche of good. This is not a laundry list of all the causes I support, and you should not feel pressure to get involved with any particular organization. Sometimes *being the change* means being the person who realizes your friend is struggling and who buys them a cup of coffee and offers an ear. We don't always have money to help people and we don't always have time to volunteer, but we can always make the world a better place in some way. And you have, I promise you. Someone's life is better because you crossed their path. Maybe you supported their local business, said something nice, or left a penny in a "take a penny, leave a penny" tray.

The world needs you. I'm glad you're in it. Together, let's make it even more amazing.

What is a kind thing you could do for someone you know who is struggling right now?

What cause speaks to your heart most? Why do you feel personally connected to it?

What is a way that
you use your time to
benefit others?

What is something
generous that someone
did for you when you
were a child?

What is your favorite
small, local business
to support?

What is a risk
you took that
ended up helping
someone else?

What is a cause you admire that you can promote (by raising awareness or giving money, time, or physical donations) today?

What is a nice thing you could do for a relative today?

Write about a
heartwarming
interaction you've
witnessed.

Who is someone
altruistic
you admire?

Have you or a loved one
ever directly benefited from
a charitable organization?
How did that feel?

What is something
kind you have done
to help a child?

What is a cause that
you wish got more
attention?

What is something
that renews your
faith in humanity?

What is the most recent
fundraising event that you
participated in? How did
it feel to be a part of it?

What is something you are very good at that could be used to help others?

_____

_____

_____

_____

What is a local organization that has had a major impact on your community?

_____

_____

_____

_____

Write about a time that you were the recipient of a random act of kindness from a friend or stranger. How did it make you feel?

What is something nice you can do on social media today?

_____

_____

_____

_____

_____

What is something simple you can do to make your home or neighborhood more pleasant for those around you?

_____

_____

_____

_____

What is the kindest thing someone has done for you that you would love to do for someone else?

What is something that renews your faith in the world?

What's a story of gratitude
you heard as a child about
a kindness that an elder in
your life experienced?

What do you feel called to do? What do you think your mission is in life?

What is something you can
do to make a difference in
one person's life?

What is something you can do
to spread awareness about a
cause you believe in?

What is a way you
can make an impact
with a decision about
where you shop or
what you purchase?

What is a cause you believe
in that you could write to your
political representatives about?
What is a change you would
like to ask them to make?

In what ways do you think
you are a positive example
for those around you?

What is something you
do for someone else that
brightens your day?

If you could give someone advice about how to really make a difference in the world, what would it be?

CHAPTER 11

outside the comfort zone

We don't necessarily want to live inside bubbles, but we all have them: areas where we tend to interact with people who are similar to ourselves in some way. That might mean most of our friends share our politics, skin color, sexual orientation, spiritual beliefs, similarities in how our bodies and neurology operate, and so on. Depending on where you live and work, you may have more or fewer interactions with people who are unlike you in some way. Then there's the Internet. It brings the whole world together and exposes us to different viewpoints. Just kidding! It certainly should, but the algorithms mostly feed us more of what we are looking for because that makes money for advertisers. So much of what we know and understand comes from our community, our environment, and our feedback loop.

Finding people with whom we relate is great. It can also be limiting. I didn't understand the intricacies of daily life for people who use mobility equipment until my mother started using a wheelchair in the late stages of her cancer. It wasn't that I didn't care before, but I suddenly became aware of the crucial importance of certain things—like easily accessible ramps and maintained and unimpeded sidewalks—in a way that was much more real and nuanced. Sometimes we simply don't know what we don't know. That's why it is important to do our research and surround ourselves with other viewpoints—without relying on marginalized people to become our educators.

Remember, it is not someone else's job to teach you what you don't know about their life. *Especially* if they are from a marginalized community. It is your job to try to learn about that community and be good to your fellow humans. For example, I know education about racism in schools has been hotly debated lately, but here's the thing: In the United States, no Black child gets the option to just "not learn about racism," even as a very small child. In fact, experiencing racism starts gut-wrenchingly early for all BIPOC kids in the United

States. For those of us who are white parents, we should want our children to also be educated about racism so that they can understand it as much as possible. Hopefully then the cycle can break.

My own experience as a lesbian mother is very similar to the experiences of many mothers, regardless of sexual orientation: My wife and I love our daughter more than life itself. We try to make sure she gets enough vegetables, we worry about her screen time, we kiss away boo-boos, we giggle over her silly stories, and we marvel at the person she is growing into with each passing year. We also worry about what people might say about her family at school or out in the world. We've had people say inappropriate things in front of her, like asking how we conceived and who her "real" mom is. The answer, of course, is that we are both her real moms. If I am not going to ask a heterosexual couple what position they were in ("doggy style or reverse cowgirl?") when they conceived their child, they shouldn't ask us about conception either. You'd think this would be obvious, but people are curious. I get it, to a point, but close personal conversations are for close personal relationships. If you haven't been let in on it in the first place, you're not close enough to ask. This obviously isn't just applicable to same-sex parents; it also goes for adoption, surrogacy, and people who don't have children.

Most of us have dealt with some area of life where we've been treated as a curiosity of sorts, some of us more than others. These comments are often from people who mean well and who want to be open and understanding, but who end up having a negative impact. As for people who say hurtful, hateful things because they have been raised in bigotry or have embraced it somewhere along the way—well, they probably aren't doing introspective journals.

For the rest of us, this chapter is a gentle way to remind us of our boundaries when it comes to those comments and to check in on our own areas where we may need some improvement.

Write about someone
you love whose
gender is different
from your own. How are
you similar? How
are you different?
What do you admire
about them?

Describe a time you disagreed with someone and it went well. Why do you think it worked out?

What is your favorite book, film, TV show, or piece of art by a person whose race is different from your own? What do you love about it?

What do you wish more
people understood about
your own life experiences?

Describe a time that you
participated in an event from
a culture or religion that is
not your own. What did you
enjoy about it? Did you learn
anything from the experience?

Who is your closest friend
or acquaintance with a
sexual orientation that is
different from your own?
How are you similar?
How are you different?
What do you admire
about them?

Describe a time when you were mocked or harmed for being different in some way and someone else stood up for you.

_____

_____

_____

_____

What is your favorite book, film, TV show, or piece of art by a person whose gender is different from your own? What do you love about it?

_____

_____

_____

_____

Write about someone you love who is from a different generation than you. What do you have in common? What is different? What do you admire about them?

What is your favorite film or
TV show about someone
whose religious or cultural
background is different from
your own? Why do you love it?

What is your favorite book, film,
TV show, or piece of art by a person
who is disabled in a way that you
are not? What do you love about it?

Who is your closest friend or acquaintance who is not the same race as you? How are you similar? How are you different? What do you admire about them?

What is something
you have learned
from someone
younger than you?

_____

_____

_____

_____

What is a culture you
would like to learn more
about? What could you
do today to start that
journey for yourself?

_____

_____

_____

_____

What is a book or film that
really opened your eyes
to an experience very
different from your own?

Write about a time that someone
you know shared a story about
their life and it made you realize
something you had never even
thought about before.

What is your favorite song by a person who is a different race from you? What about it speaks to you?

What is a way in which a close friend you love is unique and different from you?

Write about someone you love whose body shape or size is different from your own. How do you think their experience in their body is different from your experience in your body? How do you think it is similar?

What is the kindest thing a person from a significantly different background has done for you?

Write about someone you love whose spiritual beliefs are different from your own. How are you similar? How are you different? What do you admire about them?

Who is someone you care about whose political beliefs are in some way different from your own? In what areas do you agree? How are you different?

Write about a time you realized you had unintentionally said or done something that was offensive to someone else and you used it as an opportunity to grow and change.

Write about someone you love who experiences the world in some way that is different from your own. How are you similar? How are you different? What do you admire about them?

What is the biggest life lesson
you have learned from a
person who is different from
you in a significant way?

What is a song you enjoy
by someone whose sexual
orientation is different
from yours? What do
you like about it?

What is something you could do today to contribute to a cause for a marginalized community you do not belong to or amplify the voices of people in that community?

_____

_____

_____

_____

Describe a time when you stood up for yourself when someone mocked or harmed you for being different. How did it feel?

_____

_____

_____

_____

Describe a time you stood up
for someone else who was
being mocked or harmed for
being different in some way.

What is something
unique and
different about you
that you love?

CHAPTER 12

holidays
are a
mixed
bag

It's the most emotionally loaded tiiiime of the yearrrrr! I love holidays—all of them. I am the woman who would decorate and throw an Arbor Day party at the drop of the hat. I enjoy celebrating the holidays that were part of my own upbringing and sharing in the holidays that my friends celebrate. Holidays can also be a tricky time full of complicated family dynamics, societal pressure, and stress. They can remind us of losses. I remember the first Thanksgiving after I was separated from my little sisters. I was sad, the holiday was very strange, and I had no idea it would be the first of many, many Thanksgivings without them. Holidays can be about all kinds of loss and pain.

Holidays can also be whatever you want them to be! I gained a real freedom when I realized I could keep the traditions I wanted and lose what I didn't want. It was a mind-blowing revelation when I realized that I am allowed to say "no" and do things the way I'd like to for my little family.

The first time I had a "Friendsgiving" in college, it was right after my beloved roommate and long-time friend Erika was first deployed to Iraq, so we set a place at the table for her and sent her a care package. It was also the first time I realized I could do things my own way and not feel a tight ball of anxiety in my chest when I thought about holidays. I'd had so many painful holidays dealing with abuse and loss, and then this holiday was just . . . *fun*, even while I was missing the loved ones I'd lost and wishing Erika were with us. It wasn't that the bad things about life disappeared. It was just that I could acknowledge everything on my own terms. That is a lesson I hope to keep with me always, and one I want to share with you: You can do holidays *your* way.

My current holidays are all about my wife and me making our daughter's life magical and loving. We incorporate the family traditions we liked growing up and have also invented some of our own. Vivienne's best friend has two daddies and is also Jewish. So this past Christmas he came over to help us decorate our tree, and we spent the first night of Hannukah lighting candles, eating latkes, and playing dreidel with them. Hopefully this sharing of customs and family will be something they both cherish as they grow up. I thrive on spending time with friends and family, seeing my in-laws, and decorating with Cat, who is as wild about holidays as I am. You might not be that kind of person, and that is okay.

Let's acknowledge the hard things *and* embrace what fills us with comfort and joy. That's the point of this whole journal journey we've been on together. You already have the answers. Life is complicated and messy *and* you can take care of yourself on your own terms.

What is your
favorite holiday?
Why?

What is your
favorite holiday
tradition?

What is your
most profound
holiday memory,
good or bad?

What stresses you out the most around the holidays? Is there anything you can do to lessen that stress? If not, what is your best strategy for coping with it?

What is
your favorite
holiday film?

What is a holiday
tradition you wish you
had? Is it something
you could incorporate?

What makes
you feel cozy?

What is a way you can
celebrate your triumphs
from the past year?

What is one thing you could take off your holiday to-do list this year without it causing harm to yourself or anyone else? What can you just say "no" to because you don't want or need to do it?

What is a food you grew up eating around the holidays that you enjoy?

What is your
favorite
holiday song?

_____

_____

_____

_____

_____

What is the most
thoughtful holiday
gift you have ever
received?

_____

_____

_____

_____

What is a
holiday smell
that you love?

What is your
favorite holiday
decoration?

What is a holiday
activity that you
genuinely enjoy?

What is your favorite
holiday gift you
have ever given to
someone else?

What is your favorite
holiday memory from
your childhood?

_____

_____

_____

_____

What is a food you
would like to include in
a holiday celebration
but have not yet?

_____

_____

_____

What is something you
can do today to relax
and feel rejuvenated?

What is something kind
you can do for someone
else this holiday season?

Who would
you most like
to spend your
holidays with?

What is something kind
someone has done for you
this or last holiday season?

What is something
that gives you a
positive feeling of
holiday nostalgia?

What is your favorite
way to dress during
your favorite holiday?

If you could change
one thing about the way
you usually celebrate a
holiday, what would it be?

What is something
you can do today that
is just for you?

_____

_____

_____

_____

What is something you've
seen or read recently that
warmed your heart?

_____

_____

_____

_____

What makes
you feel loved?

What would you most like
to receive or be told this
holiday season?

_____

_____

_____

_____

What is something
that has recently
made you laugh?

_____

_____

_____

_____

What are you
most looking
forward to
right now?

AFTERWORD

Wow, you did it! You spent a whole year really, truly getting to know yourself and diving deep into all the ways that you are amazing. How do you feel? Did you discover anything surprising? Remember something you'd forgotten about? I hope you feel proud of yourself and all the things you have been through and survived. I hope you can marvel at the profound truths and interesting stories that have always been there with you. These fascinating answers make up who you are . . . and there is still so much more to you.

Thank you for the vulnerability. I am so grateful that you put this time and energy into exploring yourself. You are amazing, and I hope this year has confirmed that for you. Keep this book. Revisit it when you need to. Re-answer the questions as you grow and change. Mostly, hang onto it as a reminder that *you already have the answers.*

For now, I have one last question for you that you'll remember from Chapter 1:

How have you grown as a person in the last year?

I'd love it if you shared your answer with me.
Twitter: @amandadeibert
Instagram: @amandadeibertofficial

ACKNOWLEDGMENTS

This journal is the result of so many beautiful people who have touched my life. Some of them appear in this book's chapters, but many do not. I was once asked where the idea for my questions came from and at first my answer was that they just came to me on a whim, but one very introspective day I thought back to my teen years. When my mother was dying, I would stay with my best friend ReAnna and her parents Linda and Norman Farlow during my mom's weeklong chemo hospital stays. In many ways, Linda and Norman were like second parents to me. Even when I wasn't staying with them Linda would drive me to school each morning. I'd hop into the car and she'd reach her wrist over the driver's seat to the backseat, so I could rub my wrist on hers to share my Beautiful by Estée Lauder perfume. We both wore the same scent, and her bottle had broken. Then, smelling Beautiful, she would drive us to school. Before she let us get out of the car, she would ask ReAnna and me a question like "What can you do to make someone's day brighter today?" or "What is your goal for the day?" ReAnna and I would whine and try to get out of it—sometimes even jumping out of the slow-moving car when Linda told us she wouldn't stop the car until we answered—but it was always motivational and inspirational. The lesson has stayed with me for my entire life. In the absolute darkest time, there was someone who loved me enough to remind me of the power I did have: the power to answer questions, know myself better, and become the best version of me. So, first, thank you, Linda, for my questions.

Thank you also to my amazing wife Cat Staggs and our vibrant, wonder of a daughter Vivienne. I love you both beyond words. Thank you for always supporting and cheering me on. I am the luckiest woman on Earth. Thank you to my mom, Diane Postma, for your love of journals and words and, of course, for my life. I miss you always. I love you always. Thank you to my grandparents, Major John C. Deibert III and Bonnie Deibert, for being in my corner, taking in a teenager in difficult circumstances, and slaying dragons and supporting dreams from my youngest days. I love you forever. To my sisters, Jessica Postma and Katrina Postma: I love you both. I am forever sorry that our lives have had so many unfair turns. Your children are amazing and give me all the hope in the world for the future of our family, and that is a credit to you both. I can't wait to see the ways Diana, Aidan, Gabriel, and Kiernan change the world. Thank you to Norma Staggs Callahan for giving birth to the woman I married and for welcoming me so completely into this family I love. Alex Cason, thank you for being my ride or die. From kidnapping teens to moving cross-country to the million lives we've lived in between—no one else could ever have my back the way you do. McKerrin Kelly, thank you for soothing my spirit, lifting me up, and always being a safe place for me to be myself. You are my soul sister and I love you so much. Dr. Caroline Madden, this book wouldn't have happened, literally and figuratively, without you. Thank you for the love, support, encouragement, and "a room of one's own." Thank you to Jennifer Jackson, Emily Barth Isler, Jen McCreary, and Amy Preiser Moaz for the million text reassurances. Thank you to The Pile for everything. Thanks to Jane Borden for introducing me to the incredible Kristin Van Ogtrop. Thank you, Kristin, for believing in this project and helping it find the perfect home. Thank you to

Dena Rayess, Caitlin Kirkpatrick, and the entire Chronicle Books team for a match made in publishing heaven. I feel so seen and so supported. Thank you for understanding exactly the kind of power a book like this could have.

Last, and most importantly, thank you to every single person who has opened up and vulnerably shared themselves in my Twitter threads over the years. You have inspired me, awed me, made me laugh, and brought me to tears. The community we have shared these past six years brings me such joy, and I look forward to continuing to grow together with you. I love you all so much.

ABOUT THE AUTHOR

Amanda Deibert is an award-winning television and comic book writer and host of the popular podcast *Café at the End of the World* with Amanda Deibert. Her previous books include the *New York Times* bestselling series *DC Super Hero Girls*, *DC's The Doomed and the Damned*, *Teen Titans Go!*, *Batman and Harley Quinn*, *Wonder Woman '77*, *Red Sonja*, *John Carpenter's Tales for a HalloweeNight Vol. 2–7*, *He-Man and the Masters of the Universe: Legends from Castle Grayskull*, *Work for a Million*, and the *New York Times* #1 bestselling anthology *Love Is Love*. She is currently a writer for *He-Man* and *The Masters of the Universe* on Netflix.

She lives in Los Angeles with her wife Cat Staggs, their incredible daughter Vivienne, and two very cute kitties named Raven and Starfire. For more information, please visit amandadeibert.com or find her online @amandadeibert on Twitter and @amandadeibertofficial on Instagram.

Library of Congress Cataloging-in-Publication Data available.

ISBN 978-1-7972-1936-3

Manufactured in China.

Design by **VANESSA DINA.**
Illustrations by **AMBER VITTORIA.**
Typeset in TT Commons Pro.

10 9 8 7 6 5 4 3 2 1

Chronicle books and gifts are available at special quantity discounts
to corporations, professional associations, literacy programs, and other
organizations. For details and discount information, please contact our
premiums department at corporatesales@chroniclebooks.com or at
1-800-759-0190.

Chronicle Books LLC
680 Second Street
San Francisco, California 94107
WWW.CHRONICLEBOOKS.COM